EXPERT PROFILES
VOLUME 13

Conversations with Influencers & Innovators

Toni S. Winston

Patty Farmer

Dr. Terrance Cooper

Parthiv Shah

Dr. Heather Tucker

David Adelson

Jason Elias

Royalties from the Retail Sales of "Expert Profiles" are donated to Global Autism Project

AUTISM KNOWS **NO BORDERS;**
FORTUNATELY NEITHER DO WE.®

Global Autism Project 501(c)3, is a nonprofit organization which provides training to local individuals in evidence-based practices for individuals with autism.

Global Autism Project believes that every child has the ability to learn and their potential should not be limited by geographical bounds.

The Global Autism Project seeks to eliminate the disparity in service provision seen around the world by providing high-quality training to individuals providing services in their local community. This training is made sustainable through regular training trips and contiguous remote training.

You can learn more about Global Autism Project by visiting GlobalAutismProject.org.

Table of Contents

Freedom Travel
"Travel to be Free,
Be Free to Travel"

Toni Winston retired early from her position as a top performing *Benefit Client Transformation Consultant* and is now a successful owner of a lucrative travel business, Freedom Travel. She is living the life of her dreams and is a key influencer in the travel industry.

As a "tuned in" travel expert, Toni is a global connector, and the go-to person who people call to find out what is going on in the world of personal and business travel.

She has the unique ability to see and portray through a travel landscape the diversity in economic classes, different religions, contrasting beliefs, and situations that take you completely out of your comfort zone. Her zone of genius is to serve to help you better understand the world and its amazing cultures.

Toni is a contributing Amazon bestselling author of "SheCEO Let's Go!: Remove The Excuse & Stand In Your Power." She also is published in the collaborative book,

"Unselfish Women," and has been featured in the international publication, *The Global Woman* magazine.

Her expertise is seen weekly on the Celebrate You! Women Embracing Wellness Facebook Travel Thursday platform where she provides tips, tools, insights and money-making strategies for the discerning and novice traveler. She actively attends the church, where she works in her community and is a graduate of Alabama A&M University, where she is a financial alumni supporter. Toni believes that travel and adventure can be the doors to many amazing opportunities in life and in business. She leads with her signature motto, "When moving forward, never look back. The view is better from the front."

Conversation with Toni S. Winston

How did you become the Freedom Travel Diva?

Toni S. Winston: My travel business journey started with a simple invitation to attend a meeting about travel. I was working and keeping my head down about three years into a divorce. I was not feeling good about myself because my marriage didn't work out. I was beating myself up, wondering what I could have done to make it better.

Looking back, it was one simple question and one action that ended up changing my life.

A friend asked me. "Hey, don't you like to travel?" She invited me to a meeting, and within 30 minutes, I knew I had found my second niche.

Later, she asked me what I wanted to call my business. The first thing I thought was, "I'm free!" I was a middle-aged woman who was free. I was free to do whatever I chose to do. I thought, "What do people think about when they think about travel?"

"Freedom. Freedom is the whole reason people travel. It opens your eyes to different people and cultures in the world."

When you went to that meeting where the travel business opportunity was presented, what was it that inspired you to do it besides the freedom to become a travel business owner?

Toni S. Winston: Five years ago, I became a travel business owner because I can travel the world, earn commission from the trips I book and from my own trips as well. I thought if I put forth some effort, help and inspire others, build a team of like-minded people, get compensated, and earn residual income. After you get to a certain level, that residual income is like an insurance policy. If anything happens to me, my family can inherit my residual income. It just keeps coming. So, when the travel opportunity was presented, I thought about leaving a legacy to my family. It just made sense!

Looking back, I can see that my upbringing also inspired me. I can remember my parents telling me when I was a kid to try to be the best you can be and never stop learning. Those words shaped me. I get up every day with the thought, "Be the Best You Can Be! Never Stop Learning!" I read a lot about different things ranging from travel, cooking, healthy living, and football! My family encouraged me to take the initiative and to become the person I was inspired to be!

When I was 12 years old, my father asked me, "What do you want to do? Do you want to be a housewife like mom? Or do you want to go out and earn a living like I do and get a paycheck?" I opted for a paycheck. My parents instilled a strong work ethic, and taught me how to earn money, save money. My parents are in their eighties now, and I am glad they instilled those values in me as a child.

Being in the travel industry today inspires me daily to be the best I can be and never to stop learning.

How much has the COVID-19 pandemic changed the travel industry?

Toni S. Winston: COVID-19 brought everything in travel to a screeching halt. I had to cancel every trip my clients had planned for the entire year of 2020. I could not in good conscience send anyone anywhere during the pandemic. With that said, even with the cancellation of all of my client trips, since I have been part of my company I receive residual income every month. The travel business is pivoting. During this readjustment period, my company sold more than $70 million in pre-sale cruises set for 2021 and 2022 from March – June of this year. The positive thing about this for travelers is that we can set up long-term installment plans, so clients do not have to tap into their credit cards and can save that credit line for emergencies during the pandemic. It is easy to do. You can make a nominal down payment, and we will work out a payment plan that works for you with the travel supplier.

This is good for cruisers because, in most cases, depending upon the cruise line, the last payment needs to be made between 30 and 90 days before the cruise. Now is an excellent time to plan a cruise or a resort vacation for the future. There are so many options now, so it is important to plan that dream vacation. The pandemic helped the travel industry pivot and design new ways to help travelers, no matter where their destination is in the world.

Would you say that your business has thrived more than survive during this time?

Toni S. Winston: The pandemic has opened a window for me to talk to people who want more and are willing to invest in themselves. One of the things I love about my business is the challenge. I remember looking in the mirror and saying, "I have never owned a business before, but I am going to make the most of this experience."

I have never looked back! Going into the travel business is, by far, one of the best decisions I've made in the past 20 years. I love to travel! I love the life travel has helped me develop for myself! Travel has fixed my life!

How is travel affected now during times of COVID-19?

Toni S. Winston: There are travel restrictions worldwide, and many countries are closed to American citizens, just as the United States is closed to many other international citizens. The Center for Disease Control (CDC)[1] has updates regularly for traveling both domestically and internationally. There is a color rating system ranging from unknown to COVID-19 very high, similar to the terrorist ratings after 9-11.

Everyone is pivoting during this time. Travel is the No. 1 industry in the world. Everyone must do his/her due diligence and check the CDC and State Department websites for additional information. Every country and every state has its own directives, so it is vital to check it out before traveling.

What general or safety tips do you have for traveling?

Toni S. Winston: I am on speed-dial for my clients, but anyone who travels should have a checklist. I help my clients create their checklist, so they don't have to worry about anything. One of the biggest tips for any traveler is to know the rules for the airlines, cruise lines, and countries where you will travel. You must know what you can take with you when you travel. There are rules about liquids, aerosol cans, container sizes, and other items. You must check the rules and procedures. They are all different.

Travel during COVID-19 and after will be different than it was previously. Everyone will want to take precautions. I do not see masks, protective gloves, and handwashing going away any time soon.

---

[1] https://www.cdc.gov/coronavirus/2019-ncov/travelers/index.html

One of my biggest tips that will help you protect yourself and others from the virus is a $2 plastic rain poncho available at most dollar stores. The poncho fits very well over any airline seat and adds some extra protection. Don't buy a lot of expensive extra stuff. Just make sure you have your PPE (Personal Protective Equipment). I have a cloth mask with an anti-fogger in it. I also keep disposable masks. It is smart to keep extras while traveling because you may not be able to purchase these things at your destination or while traveling. Take a few minutes and think about what you need.

Start planning your travel six to nine months in advance so that you can be fully prepared. Other items to collect before travel are disposable plastic gloves, disinfectant wipes, hand sanitizer, sunblock, etc. It is easy to make your own personal kit with a heavy-duty Ziploc bag you can store in your purse or backpack.

You don't need to be afraid when you travel. Everything is sanitized regularly. Resorts and hotels, and airlines are taking extra precautions. Just relax. Enjoy yourself.

Not only are resorts and hotels taking the pandemic seriously, but they are also taking great pride in cleanliness. I just read an article about a resort in Cabo San Lucas, Mexico, about cleaning, sanitizing, and using steam to do deep cleaning of hard surfaces in the rooms and common areas. Of course, they are also using disinfectants like Lysol® and Microban® to protect against COVID.

Many resorts and hotels are creating higher standards for cleaning and sanitizing. It is a good thing. I suggest that travelers ask a travel professional like me or the resort or hotel they plan to stay about what they are doing to protect their guests. They should be able to tell you precisely what procedures they are doing to endure the utmost protection.

Another critical travel tip is to get travel insurance. In the age of COVID-19, you could test negative and be fever-free when you start your trip and end up sick when you reach your destination, so you want to be sure that you are protected so that you can get home.

What other types of travel should we expect to spike in popularity because of COVID-19?

Toni S. Winston: Domestic travel is up! There is an up-surge of families renting RVs and going to state and national parks. Believe it or not, RVs are becoming very economical for an average family of four to use. People do not need to get a huge RV; they can get a Pop-Up trailer or go luxury and find one that looks like a house inside. They are self-contained and have everything travelers would need, such as living areas, kitchens, beds, bathrooms, and showers.

The cost to stay in a state or national park is very nominal. You can get annual passes from the National Park System. Most parks are first-come, first-served, so you will need to do some planning. Some stores, including Wal-Mart, also allow RV parking in their parking lots. With some research, travelers can plan a great inexpensive vacation.

Other local trips can be fantastic, too. For example, you can take day trips and see natural wonders near your home-town. I live in Georgia, and there are 11 waterfalls within a short drive from my house. You can go now. Just take your mask and be ready in case you meet someone else on the trail.

Do you have any money-saving tips for travelers?

Toni S. Winston: There are many ways to save money on your trips. For example, some people like to go camping, but with a little glamour. They call it glamping. You can fly anywhere in the world and find glamping or camping accommodations.

There are many ways to find great deals for travel. There are hostels all over Europe and Airbnbs. There are boutique hotels nearly everywhere at reasonable rates. Whenever you travel, start with your budget and go from there.

I always ask, "What do you want to spend?" We try our very best to stick to your budget. We also make sure that our clients understand that traveling is a beautiful thing, but we've got to make sure that you have travel insurance. We cannot let you go without travel insurance. Anything can happen. I have had a client break a leg two days before traveling and could not fly. With no travel insurance, the trip went down the drain. We are pivoting and thinking outside the box in so many ways, which will help people like me, an owner/agent, help clients navigate the changes and still have the best adventure they can have in this whole wide world.

How do you work with clients? Do you work with individuals and groups?

Toni S. Winston: I created a questionnaire on my website so that anyone can get some insight. We can create short trips or longer adventures. I have worked with solo travelers, couples, and others, including families and groups like fraternities, sororities, or churches. Fill out my questionnaire on the website or talk to me. Once we have a budget, we can go from there.

You are the Freedom Travel Diva and a Freedom Ambassador; what does that mean?

Toni S. Winston: Being the Freedom Travel Diva and Freedom Ambassador means I can help others leverage their financial situation and become free. As I look back at this year of the pandemic, I see many people were not prepared. Many people did not have savings or dipped into their savings hard to survive during this time, and they do not know how they will make up that hit from using their savings to live. As a Freedom Ambassador, I can share information with others about how I was able to become free. While many people do not like to discuss finances, I want to talk to people about supplemental or primary income sources by selling travel stores nationally and internationally.

There are options out there and great resources for many to prevent the enormous rise in unemployment that we see, not only in the United States and worldwide. I want people to know that there are sources and resources out there. I took advantage of the opportunity that helped me five years ago earn residual income that continues to pay me, even in this pandemic.

With the economic uncertainties, now is an excellent time to look at different options. If anyone is interested in learning more about the travel industry as a business, I would be happy to discuss it with them directly. I want everyone to know they do not take it on the chin and lose everything or be behind the eight ball for the rest of their lives.

We no longer have to keep passing lack down through generations. There is a better way, and you do not have to change your spending habits to do it!

What is the best way to reach out to you?

Toni S. Winston: The Freedom Travel business line is (678) 235-8498.

The website is www.FreedomTravelDiva.com.

On Facebook and Instagram, it is FreedomTravelDiva.

Twitter is 1traveldiva.

The email is FreedomTravelDiva@gmail.com.

About Toni S. Winston

Toni S. Winston retired early from her position as a top-performing "Benefit Client Transformation Consultant" and is now a successful owner of a lucrative travel business. She is living the life of her dreams and is a top influencer in the travel industry.

Toni is a travel expert who is "tuned in," a connector, the go-to person who people call to find out what is going on. Her expertise comes from more than her personal and business travels.

Toni has the unique ability to see and portray through a travel landscape economic classes, different religions, contrasting beliefs, and situations that take you completely out of your comfort zone. Her zone of genius is to serve to help you better understand the world and culture.

Toni was featured as a contributing author in two books in June 2020. Amazon Best-Seller: "SheCEO Let's Go!: Remove The Excuse & Stand In Your Power."

The second being; "Unselfish Women." And she was a featured author in the Global Woman magazine, September 2020.

She is a weekly contributor for Travel Thursdays on Celebrate You! – Women Embracing Wellness, a Facebook group. She actively attends the church where she works in her community and is a graduate of Alabama A&M University, where she is a financial alumni supporter.

WEBSITE
FreedomTravelDiva.com

EMAIL
FreedomTravelDiva@gmail.com.

TELEPHONE
(678) 235-8498

FACEBOOK and INSTAGRAM
FreedomTravelDiva

TWITTER
1traveldiva

Marketing. Media. Money.

Patty Farmer is an award-winning Marketing and Media Strategist, Coach, and Business Consultant, International Speaker, Podcast Host, Magazine Publisher, and Event Producer located in Dallas, Texas. Patty works with service-based entrepreneurs, small business owners, coaches, and speakers to identify their zone of genius, target buyers, gain massive visibility, and package their knowledge into products and services while positioning them in the marketplace to maximize sales.

Patty has created a network of 100,000 + connections while teaching thousands of entrepreneurs to connect, collaborate, and convert in less time and make more money while designing the lifestyle they want to live.

Patty is passionate about helping her clients attract and convert their ideal clients to make a big impact in the world and make bigger deposits in their bank account. Patty helps her clients master their marketing, leverage the media, and monetize their business in a way that creates transformation for both them and their clients. Her mission is to help make your marketing profitable — not painful.

Patty has been seen on the covers of magazines such as Accomplish, Unleash Your Bold, Be the Boss, Women Who Mean Business, and EXPERTpreneur. She was awarded the "Global Business Strategist of the Year" by the Global Powerhouse Group in London, England, named No. 3 in the "Top Ten Media Speakers You Need to Know" and awarded "International Speaker of the Year" by the Public Speakers Association."

Patty is married to her best friend and the love of her life, and together they have raised six daughters. Patty believes that raising her daughters is the inspiration (and fortitude) that led to her passion and purpose of working with women and teaching them to empower themselves, own their voice, trust their gut, and believe in their heart that they can achieve anything they are willing to work for.

Her motto is "Lead with contribution, and compensation will follow." Her mission is to teach women that relationships are the currency in today's business environment. The key is collaboration over competition and to choose to live your life by design and with an abundance mindset.

Conversation with Patty Farmer

As an award-winning international speaker, what do you think is an essential topic your audiences should be focused on now?

Patty Farmer: Entrepreneurs, small business owners and speakers should be focusing on how to master their marketing! People must focus on and master marketing. Even more critical is once they do that, they need to know how to leverage media from both sides of the microphone. They can be both a podcast host and a guest speaker. Use both sides of the mic but remember that it is vital to master that marketing and leverage the media if you want to monetize your business.

Can you tell me a little more about your journey to becoming speaker Patty Farmer? What were some of the circumstances surrounding you the day that you said, "I'm going to become a speaker?"

Patty Farmer: I love telling the story because it even helps me to go back and remember. In 2008, I moved to the Dallas Metroplex. I didn't know anyone, not one person. As I was waiting for my furniture to be delivered, I thought to myself, "Oh my goodness, here I am in a new town, and I don't know anyone."

After I had a little bit of a pity party, I stood up, and I thought, "Patty, this is an opportunity – you're in a town where you don't know anyone, and you're in the people business."

I walked over to my refrigerator, and I wrote 100,000 on my refrigerator. When my husband got home, he said, "What is that?

I said, "I made a goal today — in one year, I will meet 100,000 business owners and entrepreneurs here in DFW. And I'm going to make a hundred thousand dollars doing it."

My husband said, "I love that goal."

I did it in nine months.

The bigger question is, how did I become a speaker? At that time, I didn't want to be a speaker. Of all the questions asked of me, I think this one is the most pivotal because I didn't want to become a speaker. I just really didn't. But somebody asked me to do it. They said, "Patty, would you come and do this? Somebody stepped out, and I need you to help me." So, I did. And here is what's funny because when I was there, as she picked me up from the airport, she said, "Oh, Patty, by the way, I know you were only going to speak for 30 minutes, but someone else got sick, and I need you to speak for an hour."

It was my very first time speaking; I was like, "what?" And then she said, "Oh, and we're going to video it."

"You've got to be kidding me," I thought. And, then my friend said, "Oh, and not only that, Patty, when you're up there, it's also okay for you to invite them into a program or something that you have." I thought, "You have got to be kidding me!"

I was so sick to my stomach. I didn't know what I was going to do. That day changed my life. That day was pivotal, pivotal to changing my life and my business. When I got there, I went to the restroom and was violently ill. I was sick for 18 months — every single time before I got on the stage — 18 months.

That day changed my life. After I spoke there, I went home and told my husband I had decided I wanted to become a speaker. I told him I would say "yes" to every opportunity that someone asked me to speak, with one caveat. I would say "yes" to talk as long as the speaking opportunity was to my ideal audience.

Two days later, I said "yes" to my first international speaking opportunity. I got on a plane and went to London to discuss using LinkedIn for lead generation. I didn't even have a speech written about that topic. I wrote the speech on the airplane. When I got there, I closed six figures and got myself booked three times in the global space. All three of the presentations were international, and I became an international speaker. London was the second time I spoke, and it changed my business forever.

What lesson have you learned from your mistakes? Is your success something that you imagined, or is it beyond what you ever imagined?

Patty Farmer: We all do make some mistakes. One of the biggest lessons I learned was that it's not that you need to reinvent ice cream; you just need to create your own flavor. And I think the most significant "aha" moment I had, especially as a speaker, was realizing that it isn't even about me. It is always about them. It's not me trying to be this eloquent speaker, wearing a soap opera dress. You know, it was really about speaking to people who needed to hear it the way I said it and taking my eyes off of me and realizing that I served them. So that was probably my biggest aha. If someone would have told me 10 years ago when I was in the bathroom being sick that ten years later, not only would I be an international speaker, but 85% of my clients would be people who are speakers that I would be helping them monetize their speaking. I would've never believed that. So, you never know.

It always starts with "yes." Then, make sure that you're saying yes to opportunities and to people who are in front of your right-fit clients and strategic partners.

Do you have any mentors or role models who have inspired you?

Patty Farmer: There's a cliche that says it takes a village to raise a child. If it takes a village to raise a child, it takes a tribe to build a business. We never get there by ourselves. We always have people who inspire and motivate us along the way. I believe with all my heart that you can't ask somebody else to invest in you if you're not willing to invest in you. So, I would say that the three people who changed my life are Jane Deuber, Ava Diamond, and Shelly Rice.

Do you have any tips about networking both in-person and online?

Patty Farmer: Networking is one of my favorite subjects.

Ask Better Questions. The first thing to do is to get rid of the "What Do You Do?" question. There are so many better questions to ask someone rather than "what do you do?" The first thing that comes to mind to ask is, "Who do you serve?" It's a much better question. Other great questions to ask include: "What's the value you bring to the marketplace?" and "What do you do differently than other people who do what you do?" Think about asking better questions!

Be Intentional. Another thing is to be intentional with your interactions and meetings. Think about it – old school net-working thinking was to go out and have coffee. The idea was that the magic happened when you were face-to-face. I don't believe that at all. How many times, whether virtually or in-person, you have ever gone and met someone for coffee and then walked out thinking, "Oh, my goodness, that's 90 minutes of my life I'll never get back!" Why? Because you didn't qualify them and have an intention for the meeting. Networking with intention is pivotal. We only have so much time – so ask better questions and then decide whether it makes sense to move forward and get together.

Can you talk more about creating solid relationships when doing business, both online and offline?

Patty Farmer: Relationships are the currency in today's business environment and the only difference between a contact and a contract is the R, and that R stands for relationships. For each person you meet, the only difference is building a relationship. And one of the things that I think is crazy in today's environment is that people believe that they're going to go from person to person thinking, "I need to pass out my business cards. I need to have this call. I need to meet this person." But the reality isn't about casting a wide net. It's about going deeper and building those relationships and knowing who they serve.

It's vital to ask yourself: "How can you go more in-depth with them and build a relationship with them and serve them in a way so that you're top of mind when they know someone who may be the right person for you to meet or serve. The reality is you make money in two ways: one is revenue, and the other is in opportunities. That's what I call OPP, which means Other People's People. You must forge a relationship with someone before asking them to put you in front of their clients, their Facebook group, or in front of an organization in which they belong. Relationships make this happen!

What social media platforms do you think are suitable for creating solid relationships?

Patty Farmer: I'm going to say that my absolute favorite social media platform is Twitter, hands down, followed by LinkedIn. And the reason why is because 78% of my closed business (sales) originates on Twitter. It doesn't always stay on Twitter, but it originates on Twitter. I teach and give workshops on Twitter. I love it.

#SocialMediaMarketingTip Spend time on the social media platform where your ideal clients and strategic partners hang out, not on YOUR favorite platform.

When you meet someone, ask them where they like to hang out. Now picture your business card in your mind. Visualize it. You have four corners on your business card. Imagine that the top right corner is Twitter; the top left corner is Instagram. The bottom right corner is LinkedIn, and the left bottom corner is Pinterest. When you meet someone, the very last question to ask them as you take their business card is, "Where do you hang out? What is your favorite social media platform?" Once you say good-bye, bend the card's corner to the social media platform the person said is their favorite. Now, you know which social media platform to connect with them. You don't need to connect on all of the platforms, only the ones where they just told you they are active on. This technique saves you time and energy. So. picture a whole stack of business cards that you collected at an event. If all you had to do was connect with that person in one place and all you have to do is look at the card, how much easier would that be? You don't have to be everywhere. You need to be where those ideal people are hanging out on social media.

The key or legend might be different for different people, but those are the four platforms that I get the most amount of business. So that's where my corners are. The four places I get the most *closed* business from are Twitter, LinkedIn, Instagram, and Pinterest, but it may be different for other people.

Can you expand on your speaking topic, "You've Got the Opt-in — Now What?"

Patty Farmer: Imagine you are in your inbox. When you open up your inbox, one finger is on the delete button as you read the subject lines. People are looking to delete emails. The opt-in is easy. But, getting people to stay with you is the hard part. You have to have a "stick" strategy. You want to have people "stick" around and stay with you to develop rapport and relationships. The first thing everyone needs to do is tell whoever opts-in what they can expect to receive because most people think, "I got what I wanted, and now I am going to unsubscribe," because they believe the next thing you will do is try and sell them something. If you do this, it is a bad practice.

The first thing I do is tell new subscribers what they can expect from me and how often they can expect to receive it. Next, I tell them the benefits of being part of the community. For example, my community's benefits might be exclusive content, deep discounts, beta testing opportunities, or other perks. I give them reasons to want to be on my list.

I make sure that I nurture and engage with them. I serve them. I also honor my subscribers by vetting them. Twice a year, I send my subscribers an email and tell them that I want to honor them by making sure that I'm only giving them information that they wish to receive, so choose the things below that you want. Then they only get the information they wish to receive.

It's important to serve, not sell. For me, if you lead with a contribution, compensation will always follow, but you always serve first.

Tell us more about Marketing, Media, and Money podcast and magazine.

Patty Farmer: Since I do marketing and media, it made perfect sense to have those assets for my clients and for the people I serve. The magazine and podcast are great resources for people who want to pick my brain. Since I can't be everywhere in person, I can be everywhere with the podcast and magazine! It's a win, win, win for everyone.

Right now, Marketing, Media, and Money magazine has more than 100,000 subscribers and is celebrating its third anniversary.

Do you have any favorite topics in the magazine or the podcast?

Patty Farmer: It's not so much that I have a favorite topic per se, but my three favorite words are strategy, leverage, and monetize. Topics that focus on those three things make me happy. The most important thing to me in both the magazine and podcast is to provide strategies and tactics that work now. It is important to know what is working currently, not what worked five years ago or even two years ago. We want to share what's working NOW to help people grow, build, and scale their businesses.

Following up on the concept of 'What's working now?"
What are you working on now and in the future?

Patty Farmer: I typically produce about five live events each year, but since I cannot do any of my live events or my flagship in-person event in New York this year, we are pivoting to doing more virtual events. For me, it is about "how can I serve?" I plan to roll out a second magazine and podcast, and I am producing a marketing, media, and money mastermind specifically for podcasters and another for speakers. I am also taking time to finish my book.

What do you think is the most important thing anyone can do right now?

Patty Farmer: There are a couple of essential things. The first thing is to make sure they stay in their lane. I think it is a temptation right now for people to be all over the place with products and services. I think spreading yourself out too thin confuses people. It distracts people. It can give people the wrong message. My advice is to sit down and take inventory of your strengths and then focus on those strengths. I truly believe that you should work in your brilliance and hire other people to work in theirs. I think many times, people think they don't want to hire anyone. I believe this is when you should be very strategic and know your strengths as well as the things you may not be as strong in or don't like to do. Once you have your strengths, ask yourself, what else can I do to serve and support my ideal clients, strategic partners, and my network.

And whether that is creating new products or services, changing up your pricing strategy, whatever the case may be, this is the time to hire someone who can help you if you can't do it on your own. If there's ever been a time, this is not the time to say, "Oh, I'm not going to hire anyone or spend any money." This is the time to be very strategic. If you're not a master marketer, hire someone who is. If you're not good at media, hire someone. If you need branding help, if you're not good at social media, find someone who can help. You know your strengths, and you know where you need assistance, so hire someone to help you.

How do you work with your clients? Can you outline what that looks like?

Patty Farmer: I always start with a conversation about lifestyle. Most of us get into business for ourselves to live a particular lifestyle. For me, everything is about time freedom. Ask yourself the question, "What is the lifestyle I want to live?" I always start with that because some people might want to take 10 vacations a year, and someone else might want to be able to every day get off at 3 pm and go to their kid's soccer games. It's not the same for everybody. The first thing for me is always; let's talk about the lifestyle that you want. Let's design that. And then I will help you build a business that will support that lifestyle, not the other way around.

So that's the beginning. The end goal is always to make the business profitable, but it's also to create transformation. Not just for the individual, but their clients as well. I'm not in the information business; Google is in the information business. I'm in the transformation business. My end goal is always to help my clients transform their personal lives, business, and clients. There is no one size fits all. But one of the most important things to me is understanding how my clients want to serve and to identify gaps and fill them with time or money.

It is important to understand the gaps. For example, many people are doing many things, but they don't know how to package themselves. They don't know how to package their services or their products. They don't use the right pricing strategy. And most importantly, they don't know how to position themselves in the marketplace correctly. We work on their business from all angles. In the end, it always a transformation for them and their clients.

To get a taste of how I work with my clients, an excellent place to start is the Marketing, Media, and Money assessment https://M3BizQuiz.com

How can the Marketing, Media, and Money Assessment help your potential clients or your clients?

Patty Farmer: In three minutes or less, someone will know where they are excelling in seven key areas. This assessment can help someone understand what they do well and where they can make some changes. It includes the next steps for massive action that gets tremendous results. Even if they never hired me or contacted me again, I created a resource that would serve them. You can ask yourself the big question: Is my marketing profitable or painful? Anyone interested can take the quiz at https://M3BizQuiz.com It's free.

How can people reach out to you?

Patty Farmer: Visit https://PattyFarmer.com. You can find information about the magazine and podcast there as well as other free resources and you can grab your FREE lifetime subscription to the magazine at MarketingMediaMoney.com.

About Patty Farmer

Patty Farmer is an award-winning Marketing and Media Strategist, Coach, and Business Consultant, International Speaker, Podcast Host, Magazine Publisher, and Event Producer located in Dallas, Texas.

Patty works with service-based entrepreneurs, small business owners, coaches, and speakers to identify their zone of genius, target buyers, gain massive visibility, and package their knowledge into products and services while positioning them in the marketplace to maximize sales.

Patty has created a network of 100,000+ connections while teaching thousands of entrepreneurs to connect, collaborate, and convert in less time and make more money while designing the lifestyle they want to live.

WEBSITE
PattyFarmer.com

EMAIL
patty@pattyfarmer.com

QUIZ
https://M3BizQuiz.com

FACEBOOK
Facebook.com/NetworkingCEO

TWITTER
Twitter.com/masterthemic

MAGAZINE SUBSCRIPTION
MarketingMediaMoney.com

How a Whole Body Vibration Machine Made for Seniors Helps the Body Heal Itself

Dr. Terrance Cooper (affectionately called Doc by his patients) spent 43 years as a Chiropractic Physician. When he retired from full time practice in 2017, he didn't retire from helping patients with natural healing methods.

In this interview Dr. Cooper shares how a whole body vibration machine called the Lifetime Vibe is helping seniors regain their health, increase their mobility and give them hope for less pain.

Conversation with Dr. Terrance Cooper

What is your personal experience using the LifetimeVibe whole body vibration machine?

Dr. Cooper: I had Plantar Fasciitis for over nine years. I would have to have cortisone shots in my foot for the pain. As bad it sounds, it was even worse. It would help for a few days, but it would wear off and the pain was excruciating. I was facing the rest of my life in a wheelchair. A friend of mine, Vickie Honey, told me about a vibration machine she was selling. She told me stories of how it helped people, so I thought why not give it a try. It's been nine years and I've haven't had any more shots in my foot and I never became wheelchair bound. At 79 years old, my health is excellent.

What other health issues have you seen that have been resolved with LifetimeVibe?

Dr. Cooper: I have many case studies with arthritis, balance, cellulite, constipation, diabetes, lower back pain, fatigue, fibromyalgia, incontinence, dizziness, osteoporosis, poor circulation, varicose vein, and much more. Here's just a few stories.

When Jim, an 80-year-old man in St. George, Utah, walked, he had lower back pain, limped, and drug his right leg. After using the machine for three weeks, his lower back pain subsided, but he still had pain in his leg. I called Jim three months later and he said he was 100% pain free, his leg no longer hurt him, nor did he limp.

I have in my hand an unsolicited letter from an 80 plus year old man named Mac from Naples, Florida. He said,

"I was diagnosed with Parkinson's disease in 2009. I took the standard medication and exercise programs for the next five years. After five years my condition worsened to the degree more medication was required and daily exercise became problematic due to severe drops in blood pressure, lack of balance, and sore and stiff joints. I was suffering more pain, lack of sleep, disturbing shifts in vision, and constant constipation.

In December 2015, I discovered a vibration machine made especially for seniors. I bought the LifetimeVibe and ever since, my life has had a rather miraculous recovery from some of the symptoms of Parkinson's disease. Within two weeks, I started to realize the benefits of this wonderful machine.

- *First thing I noticed was a marked improvement in my balance.*

- *Then my constipatio diminished.*

- *I felt my muscle tone was returning and my blood pressure was stabilizing.*

- *I also began to achieve normal sleep pattern. I was getting 5-7 hours of sleep when I used to only get three hours."*

Unfortunately, LifetimeVibe is not a cure for Parkinson's disease. However, anyone who is going through the disruption of their life caused by this disease has a chance to greatly increase their quality of life through its use.

Lady in California:

- She had a Herrington steel Rod surgically implanted in her back for a severe curvature of her spine. The pain was so excruciating that she had it removed.

- She bought the LifetimeVibe machine and hoped it would help strengthen her back.

- When I called her, she was ready to send the machine back.

- She said using the machine only made her hurt worse. I asked her how she was using the machine. She told me what she was doing and everything she was doing was wrong.

- I then told her how to use the machine and I put her on an exercise program which would strengthen her spine.

- I called her every three days for her progress, and in two weeks, she was thrilled with her results. Her back was getting stronger and she was having less pain.

Man in Luis Obispo, California:

- Roger had low back surgery and was suffering with continuing back pain.

- I sold him his machine and he was so excited to use it. I told him before he started to use his machine that he was to call me.

- He got the machine and was going to stand on it, but he called me, and I told him that was the worst thing he could do for his condition.

- He started out by sitting on the machine and immediately noticed relief in his lower back. Both he and he wife now use the machine daily.

Gayle from my office in Parowan:

- Her mother was 90 years old and she had problems in her legs. They were blue from the top of her knees to the bottom of her feet due to poor circulation. She also had a balance issue and some dementia.

- She and her sister bought her mother a machine.

- I didn't want her to stand on the machine, so we had her sit in front of the machine with her feet on the plate.

- In three weeks, we had her standing on the machine doing exercises.

- Three months later when she went to see her Medical doctor in Parowan, her legs were normal and there was no blueness and Dr. White was amazed. He told her since he had been treating her, she had congestive heart failure for the past 20 years. Her lungs were now clear.

Husband and Wife: Idaho

- Lynn and Cathy: Both were having lower back pain and were seniors.

- They bought the LifetimeVibe machine. Lynn was having neck pain along with muscle spasms in his shoulders and back pain.

- I had him do the exercises in the booklet for shoulder and neck pain. He did it two times daily and he was doing wonderful. His back pain completely cleared up.

- Cathy was 100% out of pain.

Husband and wife: Brigham City, Utah

- Jim and Randa: Jim was having swollen feet and difficulty with his balance.

- Randa was having right leg and lower back pain.

- They bought the LifetimeVibe machine and Jim has noticed a reduction of swelling in both of his feet and he has an improvement in his balance.

- Randa who was having back pain with muscle spasms is doing wonderful. They use the machine two and sometimes three times a day.

Husband and Wife: Malad, Idaho

- Julie and Dan: Julie was having lower back, hip pain, and swollen feet.

- Dan said he didn't particularly have any problems.

- She bought the machine and got immediate relief and then Dan started using it. He thought he was feeling good until he used her LifetimeVibe and he felt so much better.

- They were so excited they invited their neighbors to come over and use their machine.

How does a simple machine you stand on a few minutes a day help so many different health challenges?

Dr. Cooper: The first thing anyone will notice immediately when standing on the LifetimeVibe is the smooth and gentle speed as it immediately relaxes your muscles. It stimulates your lymphatic system, and the lymphatic system is what flushes out the toxins from the body. The only way the lymphatic system works is when you exercise. But for most people who are hurting, they can't do exercises when they are in pain. When you stand on the Lifetime vibe for ten minutes it's like exercising for an hour.

- It stimulates your organs, muscles, and nervous system
- Increases blood flow to all areas of your body
- Relieves stress in your body
- Increases joint flexibility

What if someone can't stand on it for ten minutes?

Dr. Cooper: This is one thing that is different from any vibration machine in the world. You don't always have stand on the machine. We have a stool that comes with the machine so seniors can sit down and do specific exercises. We have added rails on the side of the machine to help them sit down and to help them stand up. It is the only one in the world that has these added features.

- If you have tightness or spasms in your shoulders or neck: There is a wonderful exercise takes the stress away. That is my favorite. You kneel in front of the machine with your hands on the plate. With the gentle motion of the machine, it relaxes your shoulders and neck. I use this all the time.

- The machine has 12 different programs that are programmed into the machine for specific problems. One is stimulation of the lymphatic system, another is relaxation.

- We have an easy-to-use manual that comes with every machine and what to do for pain you are having in different areas of your body.

- One side of the booklet deals with health issues, the other side deals with exercises. It's very comprehensive easy to follow with examples and pictures.

Tell me more about how the machine works

Dr. Cooper: The machine's plate that you stand on has an oscillating motion, which simulates as if you are walking. When you stand on the plate, the first thing you'll feel is the smooth and gentle action of the machine which creates a wonderful sensation from your toes to the top of your head. If you have swelling in your legs, knees, or ankle, it takes ways the swelling.

One of my patients from Virginia has acute Lymphedema in her both of her legs. She had tried everything from medication, special creams to Epson salts baths with no success. She purchased the LifetimeVibe machine in early October of 2020. I told her to use the machine two minutes every ½ hour for at least a week. It may take her at least 3-4 weeks, but she has had this problem for over a year. I call her every two days to see how she is doing. She told me she used to cry herself to sleep because of the pain. I have made some changes in how she should use her machine, and she is feeling much better and is so grateful for the machine.

How did you become acquainted with the LifetimeVibe machine?

Dr. Cooper: My chiropractic practice was in Parowan, Utah, which is a small town. My friends owned the Main Street Gym. They had bought a vibrating machine for their gym users. I sent my senior patients over to the gym to use their new vibration machine to help strengthen their bodies. Everyone came back complaining that after using the machine their knees and joints hurt because the machine's plate that they stood on was so violent. I went to the gym and used the machine myself. They were right. It was very harsh and extremely powerful when using it. Their exercise machine was made for athletes and younger adults who wanted to tone their bodies and work out. But for an older person's body, it was too harsh. While attending a Chiropractic Seminar, I met Vicki Honey. She was selling a vibrating machine that she bought out of Canada, and it was imported from China. I started selling her machine to my patients, but soon we started having problems.

What type of problems?

Dr. Cooper: The machine was too abrasive on my patients. It was even worse than the one at the gym. After using the new vibration machine, some of my patients complained that their feet and knees hurt. Some patients who had pain in their hips and low back said it only increased their pain. This machine also was just too powerful. The machine's plate, which my patients stood on, was 12 inches off the floor. For some seniors, it was too high for them to lift their legs up to stand on, especially if they had pain in their lower back. And there was nothing to hold on to while standing on the machine, except a side bar. It would not work on carpet, and the machine would shake violently. Hardwood floors or concrete floor were the only thing that the machine could be used on. Some of the machines broke down and we could not get them fixed, and there was no guarantee. We couldn't send them back to Canada or China to have them fixed.

Vicki, who was a senior herself, became so disgusted with the Chinese machines that she decided to manufacture a vibration machine of her own. She found a great engineer and a little under two years, she had her own machine and she made it especially for seniors. She called it the LifetimeVibe because it can be used for a lifetime.

With your experience over the years, what have you noticed about other machines made in China?

Dr. Cooper: Overall, most Chinese machines are well made, but every machine I have tried is very vigorous and powerful. They are made to strengthen, tone, and condition athletes or younger adult's bodies. But when it breaks (and they often do), there is no getting them fixed. None of them are made for seniors. There are no rails in the front, no way to use them sitting down, they start with a jerk rather than smoothly, and too high off the ground.

When Vicki manufactured her machine, it was completely different from any Chinese machine on the market, or in the world. It was made from the ground up here in Utah with seniors in mind.

- The LifetimeVibe's plate action is smooth and gentle on a senior's body. Those with pain in their bodies, or health conditions will immediately notice a feeling of wellbeing from the bottom of their toes to the top of their head.

- When the machine starts it slowly works up to the speed and when it shuts down it gently slows down before stopping. There is no sudden start up with no jarring.

- It was built six inches off the ground. Easy for anyone to stand up on.

- It has a stool to sit and exercise on and side rails to help seniors sit down and stand up.

- It's made in America.

- There is a 5-year guarantee on the motor and parts replacement for two years.

- They have a satisfaction and money back guarantee.

- Anyone can use it for two weeks and if not satisfied, they will even pay for return shipping.

What role do you play as the Consulting Physician?

Dr. Cooper: My role is to make sure everyone who buys the machine knows exactly how to use it for their condition. Yes, there is a manual, but I know seniors most appreciate a personal touch and someone to talk to. I've helped hundreds of people with their problems. They would never get that personal help from any Chinese machine.

If someone would like to talk to you about the LifetimeVibe Machine, what's the best way to connect?

Dr. Cooper: They can call me at 435-531-9418 or email me at doctmcooper@yahoo.com.

About Dr. Terrance Cooper

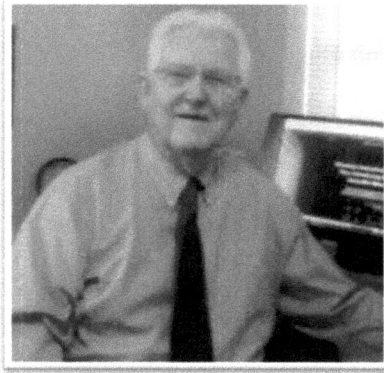

Doc Cooper practiced Chiropractic for 43 years in California and Utah. He retired from his chiropractic practice in 2017 but not from helping seniors regain their health through natural means when possible. While he is not adjusting his patients full time, he can't stop himself from being passionate about their health.

He is now the consulting Physician for LifetimeVibe – a company in Orem, Utah - who manufactures the LifetimeVibe Senior Exercise Machine. He knows first-hand the power of whole body vibration when his Plantar Fasciitis was resolved when he began to use the machine nine years ago.

Today, he spends hours a day on the phone with patients from all over the world to be sure they understand how to use the LifetimeVibe Machine.

WEBSITE: https://lifetimevibe.com/

EMAIL: doctmcooper@yahoo.com

PHONE: 435-531-9418

How to Pivot During the COVID Crisis and Over the Next Several Years

Over 300 dentists, physicians and other clients from 27 states in USA and over eight other countries have benefited from working with Parthiv and eLaunchers.com. As with most businesses, when COVID hit in March of 2020, eLaunchers saw their business tumble by 85%.

Born and raised in India, Pathiv is no stranger to figuring out a pivot plan in his life. He came to America at the age of 21 (33 years ago) and had to create his own life's success plan. Known for his ability to see a problem and create a strategy for success, 2020 put all his knowledge with his own business and his client's businesses to the test. But as a master of direct response marketing, Parthiv and his clients not only got through the crisis, but they are beginning to thrive again.

Conversation with Parthiv Shah

Tell us about your business and who your clients are

Parthiv Shah: My company, eLaunchers, serves businesses that make money by appointment (dentists, pain management clinics, physicians, financial advisors, attorneys, coaches/ consultants, information marketers).

How was 2019 and what were the projections for 2020?

Parthiv Shah: 2019 was the best year we ever had. It was our first 7-figure year. 2020 projections were looking good until COVID hit in March. 85% of eLaunchers monthly revenues were wiped out within three days in March. This tested the strength of our savings account.

What did you do?

Parthiv Shah: Clinics and businesses were shutting down. Everyone was cutting back and no one had any money to spend on anything. But business had to go on.

We did THREE main things:

1. Those who did not pay our monthly fees, we continued to work for them anyway. Whatever was not paid, we simply wrote it off, but we never stopped working.

2. We started giving away our intellectual property to anyone who asked. We gave away free funnels, free campaigns, free swipe files, free copy/content bank -

free everything. I also conducted over a hundred free consultations on helping people pivot.

3. We launched 'eLaunchers Coronavirus Economic impact Recovery Plan for Dentists.' We teamed up with 'Dental Intel' – a dental software company.

We helped dentists identify specific business opportunities from within their internal database and created processes to stay in touch with those specific patients.

We developed 'smile books,' a packet of digital case studies that the dentist can use for case presentation during online consultations.

We converted many of our signature tools from print to digital and started giving those away.

What we did for dentists worked in every one of our other client businesses.

How quickly did it take to get results?

Parthiv Shah: We declared June as 'Post-COVID month.' It's a mindset, and we decided to change that mindset. The elongated 'COVID economics' are here to stay for the next two to four years, but the market now knows about it. The most painful part of a trauma is not the impact or the pain, but the surprise. When you know you are going to get hit by an impact, you can actually do something about it. Defensive marketing strategies were developed and deployed with all our clients.

In our business, we stopped losing money in August. We reached pre-COVID revenues in October. Now we're back to focusing on growth again.

That is for your own company, how about your clients?

Parthiv Shah: Same scene, same story.

What will be the impact of the election be on your business and business of your clients?

Parthiv Shah: Nothing will change. It does not matter who wins the election. The dollar will always remain in power. There is NOTHING happening from any force that weakens the buying power of the dollar.

A strong downward drift on economies will continue for the next two to four years for sure, forcing economic problems, but the crisis is gone. Now we just have one large, prolonged, but manageable problem.

So how do you 'manage' this problem?

Parthiv Shah: I am 54 years old. COVID is not the first blunt economic traumatic impact I have seen in my life. We saw this exact thing in post dot-com bust, post 9-11, after the battle of Tora-bora in Afghanistan, after the Iraq war, and after the mortgage meltdown in 2008.

What was common among those economic events?

Parthiv Shah: The base was compromised. Marketing budgets were wiped out, marketing teams were laid off. Sales teams were demoralized. Half or more customers and associated revenues were gone. What little was left was fiercely poached by competitors.

But it was not all reduced to ZERO. It was all reduced to NEAR ZERO.

And as long as you have LITTLE BIT OF WIND, the plane can still fly. It just needs more energy, and it needs to be able to travel at low velocity. (It does not quite work that way for airplane, but fortunately, business is not a plane. This actually works in business.)

So, what are companies supposed to do at this time?

Parthiv Shah: At times like this, you need to compromise your brand development efforts and divert your marketing energy towards transaction focused, direct response marketing. This is the time for highly targeted, multi-step direct mail marketing and long-term nurture for unconverted leads, lost opportunities and lost clients.

At times like this, you want to identify pockets of opportunities in your business and strike where you are likely to win.

What are businesses supposed to do if they don't have money?

Parthiv Shah: Welcome to the club. We all have the same problem. I don't have money either.

Fortunately, your competitors don't have money either.

You will need to be smart about your spending and spend what little you have on marketing efforts that actually matter.

It's not that you have zero money. You have NEAR ZERO money. There is a BIG difference.

So, what do brands do with near zero money?

Parthiv Shah: Historically, larger brands have hired smaller agencies in down market trends.

Focus has shifted to small quantity, multi-step direct mail marketing with a long form sales letter.

Those who can't afford that will resort to telemarketing, small budget digital marketing (paid, online advertising) and multi-step email marketing.

What are YOU doing to grow eLaunchers? You can't be exhibiting at events, which was your MAIN lead generation activity?

Parthiv Shah: Yeah, the large, on-ground events are gone. No more exhibit booths, grand dinner with Dan Kennedy, or large chocolate reception at the booth.

But there are still events online. We sponsor those. I speak at small online conferences, give value, share THIS story on what the brands can do with their now tiny marketing budget, and share resources. Most people take our gifts. Some of them hire us to turnkey the programs.

Give me the numbers. What's going on at eLaunchers?

Parthiv Shah: The cost per lead has gone up 300%. Lead to interview has gone down 50%. Interview to close has gone down 50%. Close to ascension has gone down 50%. Compounding effect of COVD economics is non-trivial. I need 5X the number of leads for every $1,000 dollars spent.

So, what are you going to do about it?

Parthiv Shah: We send out five to ten FedEx packages each day. My main sales letter is performing VERY WELL. It was written by my chief copywriter Russell Martino and curated or critiqued by Dan Kennedy. Dan and Russell worked on this letter together.

There is a series of four additional FedEx packages that go out to those who don't respond to FedEx package #1.

We have a large push to get affiliates/centers of influence to promote our message to their tribe. Coaches, consultants, tribe leaders and info-marketers are introducing us as the 'survival team' to their coaching and mastermind members.

What does 2021 looks like?

Parthiv Shah: It appears that the bad days are behind us. We are either running out of things that can go wrong, or I am in between problems… but today is a good day.

What advice would you give to businesses out there?

Parthiv Shah: Don't lose hope. Have faith. The worst of this storm is now behind you. If you are still alive, it can only get better from here. If your business died, start a new one.

For the next two to four years, we are going to be in a suppressed economic environment with most people in economic pain and distress. These are opportune times for entrepreneurial people. This is just like the prior economic impacts: (dot-com bust, 9-11, wars, mortgage crisis in 2008). Direct response thrives under conditions like this.

If someone would like to talk to you about helping them with their business, what's the best way to connect?

Parthiv Shah: Go to www.eLaunchers.com/start. They'll find a specific marketing plan to help them in their business. If it makes sense we talk after reading that 20-page report, then we can schedule a free 20-minute call.

About Parthiv Shah

Parthiv Shah is the Founder and President of eLaunchers.com. Over 300 dentists, physicians and other clients from 27 states in USA and over eight other countries have benefited from working with Parthiv and eLaunchers.com.

He is the author of his International Bestselling book, "Business Kamasutra," and is a contributor or co-author to six additional books. His upcoming book 'Copy That Sells' is co-authored with marketing legend Dan Kennedy. He is routinely invited to speak as technology expert at direct marketing conferences and small group mastermind sessions.

Parthiv received his MBA in 1994. He has worked on over 10000 direct mail marketing projects and mailed over a billion pieces of direct mail. He is a veteran of the Indian Air Force, member of the Lions Club, a Leadership Montgomery Core Program graduate (class of 2016) and the proud dad of an Eagle Scout.

eLaunchers was named Small Business of The Year in 2016 and inducted into the GKIC Direct Response Hall of Fame in 2017. They are a GKIC Certified Magnetic Marketing Advisor (2010), Infusionsoft Certified Partner (2011), Digital Marketer Certified Partner (2014), Click Funnels Certified Partner

(2015) and Hubspot Certified Partner (2017). In addition, Parthiv is trained on Salesforce.com, ZOHO, Microsoft Dynamics and six other cloud based and desktop CRM systems.

WEBSITE
www.eLuanchers.com

EMAIL
PShah@eLaunchers.com

Lean In. Let Go. Leap Forward.

Dr. Heather Tucker was making six figures in her dream job when she realized that the pressure, lack of recognition and support, and disruption of family engagement had turned her into somebody she didn't know. That's when she called a halt and redesigned her life around who she really is. The life harmony that she found in her own life is what she teaches others.

In 2018 alone, Dr. Heather certified more than 300 life coaches who spread the message of empowerment. She teaches her students solid methods on how to stress less, strengthen their relationships, and make more money so they can lead with more momentum in their personal and professional lives. Dr. Heather's primary areas of expertise include leadership, relationships, emotional intelligence, trauma and Post-Traumatic Stress Disorder (PTSD), technology harmony, and business building.

Dr. Heather has more than 15 years of higher education teaching and research experience as well as a natural gift of easily working with others.

She received her Ph.D. and Master's in Information Systems (Human-Computer Interaction) at age 27 from the

University of Maryland Baltimore County. She also has a Bachelor of Science degree in Computer Science from the University of Maryland Eastern Shore. Dr. Heather's work has been published in many peer-reviewed journals, conference proceedings and books.

Now, Dr. Heather is happily married to her husband Winston "Tuck," and loves being mommy to son, Noah, and daughter, Alyssa. She is living the business and life harmony she always wanted.

Conversation with Dr. Heather Tucker

What does Life Harmony mean?

Dr. Heather Tucker: Life Harmony has to do with paying attention, having awareness, and being at peace on all sides of life – health, relationships, family, career, business, financial, etc. — these areas can pull on us at times causing overwhelm and stress. For example, have you ever been so overwhelmed that all life areas were on red alert, and perhaps you got frozen and couldn't move forward? Perhaps, you felt defeated, stuck, and just wanted to give up and say, "You know what—I'm done!"

The reality is the only constant is change. Many times, it's difficult for us to be able to pivot when something happens. Things can happen unexpectedly, like a loved one could get sick, or a loved one could pass away, or other "life" things, such as a breakup or divorce or loss of a job.

In 2020, this whole pandemic and everything else we have experienced has caused people to be overwhelmed and stressed out to the max. We've were forced to figure out how to manage and juggle so much simultaneously. In this time both work and family collided, we lost so many good people.

The core of Life Harmony is Emotional Intelligence. We can't control how other people act or the significant emotional events that happen around us, however, we can control how we respond to it. It's about having peace and power, even in the midst of the chaos. It is about tapping into our unlimited supply of Aloha and support as we're operating or navigating through life's situations.

Can you tell me more about life coaching and emotional intelligence and the connection?

Dr. Heather Tucker: Many of us have been taught not to express our emotions or feelings and to rely on the more logical aspect of our mind. We can develop a tendency or pattern of stuffing down and ignore our feelings. We tend to suppress our emotions, especially the negative ones, oftentimes for survival purposes. However, feelings can remain in our mind and body, and come out at unwanted time and in undesirable ways, behaviors, relationship difficulties, overreactions, addictions, conflicts. When it comes to emotional intelligence, that is the core of not allowing other people or our external environment to impact our internal condition. Why is this so important? For our own health, and the health of our loved ones. Stress is very contagious, especially for those who are sensitive to energy and emotions. This can have a negative impact on our personal and professional relationships. When it gets so heavy, it's easy to want to give up and throw in the towel. Right now, there is a higher suicide rate, higher divorce rate, higher death rates, and we are all so divided when we are called for unity. There is hope and a solution, and that is learning how to master your communication and life coaching with emotional intelligence.

Life coaching is a powerful practice of allowing someone to express and breakthrough difficult situations and guiding them to where they want to be. Life coaching also produces a positive ripple effect into the client's personal and professional relationships. In our communication mastery training, we learn how to empower our mind and strengthen the relationships and connection with God, ourselves, and others. One of our principles on how to successful people operation is to respect people's model of the world, even if we don't agree with it. It is about becoming united, internally and externally, instead of divided or conflicted. One of the reasons I started on this journey was that I had reached a popping point in my own life. I had the perfect dream job, a six-figure position, and I was headed up the ladder. While I was success-ful externally, internally, I was in misery. On the outside, people see that everything is OK, but inside there was a tug-o-war. When there's conflict inside, there's also going to be conflict externally.

Tell us more about why and how you extricated yourself out of that six-figure, dream job to become who you are today?

Dr. Heather Tucker: It was about letting go. To become who you're called to be, you have to let go of everything you think you are. There are three representations of us: who we are, who we think we are, and who others think we are. For me, they were all conflicting in my life. I had real problems in my personal and intimate relationships, and the outside world was in turmoil. The straw that broke the camel's back for me for what happened to Trayvon Martin. He was the same age as my nephew, and I knew I could no longer sit back in this cushy position and not be part of the solution.

Like when, and of course, all the incidences that happened after that, they used to take me away, emotionally. We see so many women, especially women of color, who are crying out in concern for their kids. I have a son and a daughter, and I'm concerned about their legacy and what they're going to exper-ience in the world. I want to make sure they have the most positive experiences as possible. All of this negativity used to take me down emotionally, but now I recognize that I'm part of the solution and I stand firm when similar experiences happen. We can't control things that happen, but we can control how we respond to them. This realization led me to understand it was time to fulfill my purpose in the world.

When you speak, what are some of your favorite topics?

Dr. Heather Tucker: The most significant talk we have is *Peace Under Pressure*, where I share the five secrets to creating ultimate biz/life harmony or work/life harmony.

Some of the biggest stressors in our business and home life are created by the emotional responses that ripple out to those around us, causing even more stress. By learning how to manage our own emotions and stress levels, we can dial down the drama in our lives, whether health, relationships, or business.

In this talk, I show how to achieve peace, even with pressure at work, by creating life harmony so that you manifest supportive environments rather than ones that produce friction.

The goal is to help people feel secure, supported, and successful, both inside and out. It's about letting go and leaping forward in your destiny with more ease and love. The goal is to eradicate painful challenges so that there is more confidence, clarity, and consistency.

Another talk I enjoy giving is Culture By Design: Magical Secrets to Creating a Confidently Connected Team. Who says you can't have it all? I share powerful insights on creating a team that feels like a family where all members feel valued, secure, and supported without judgment. Imagine the joy and connection from a team or family operating on one accord towards a desired mission and vision. When a workplace, business culture, or home environment is well-designed, it can increase satisfaction and productivity all around.

What are some of the courses and programs you are planning now?

Dr. Heather Tucker: We offer two certification trainings to renew your mind, body, and soul, so that you can fully walk in your purpose. The Life Harmony Coach Certification Training is a program designed to provide solid coaching knowledge, skills, and applied practice to develop a thriving coaching practice and expand an existing business's services. The Communication Mastery Certification® Training Event is a five-day interactive and experiential program that provides proven tools and techniques using NLP (Neuro-Linguistic Programming).

Go to https://www.anotherlevelliving.com/trainings

We also offer speaking and coaching services as well.

You have written several books. Can you tell us more about your book projects?

Dr. Heather Tucker: The first book I ever wrote was my dissertation. It was on teachers' technology acceptance and usage behavior of the interactive job-related technologies they had available. I was a contributing author for *Destiny Walkers*. It is a book about how to walk in your calling.

My most prized possession is the book collaboration and book series I started called the *Voice of Hope* (VoiceofHopeBook.com). It's inspirational stories for caregivers by caregivers. As caregivers, this book helps us see our burdens as blessings aiding our transformation.

Are you working on any new book projects?

Dr. Heather Tucker: Currently, I am working on the second volume of *Voices of Hope.* I also am working on another book about becoming a warrior. Right now, everyone desires acceptance and connection. This book is for coaches or entrepreneurs who are working toward their dreams, even though there are so many obstacles and hills and valleys that they have to climb and walkthrough. In this book, people will share their journeys, so other people know that others have been through it, too. It's about transformation, and the blessings that come after the process is complete.

You were in Hawaii recently, is there anything you have learned from the Hawaiian culture?

Dr. Heather Tucker: Many, many things which is why in just a few months, we are launching our Aloha mastermind. It is an Ohana (the Hawaiian word for family) for coaches and practitioners. Not only will we be teaching coaches and practitioners, but we will provide a supportive community for them to continue as they evolve, arise, connect, stand in their power, and unleash their greatness with ease.

What advice do you have for anyone who is thinking about becoming a coach?

Dr. Heather Tucker: I just wanted to say for whoever's listening to this recording or reading the profile and the book that no matter who you think you are you're so much more than that. And some people are waiting for you to be able to show up and step into everything that you've been called to be. If you read this message and you're like, you know, I'm ready to make a difference and be of service to others. I'm prepared to be able to be the one and inspire other people. Don't listen to the self-doubt chatter that discourages you from stepping up and serving in your light. The truth is that you only need to be just one step ahead to be a fantastic coach.

How can people contact you? Do you have some gifts for them?

Dr. Heather Tucker: Visit AnotherLevelLiving.com. You can sign up to receive some gifts there, too. Also, connect with me on social media.

About Heather Tucker, Ph.D.

Dr. Heather Tucker guides business leaders to stress less, make more money, and strengthen their relationships. She is uniquely skilled in the areas of technology interaction, post-traumatic stress disorder (PTSD), and emotional intelligence. Her clients receive rapid results in their professional and personal lives. They are then able to lead with more momentum and peace of mind.

WEBSITE
AnotherLevelLiving.com

EMAIL
heather@AnotherLevelLiving.com

LINKEDIN
LinkedIn.com/in/DrHeatherTucker

FACEBOOK
Facebook.com/AnotherLevelLiv

INSTAGRAM
Instagram.com/AnotherLevelLiv

Peace and Harmony Now

David Adelson believes that life's purpose is the expansion of happiness, and that belief started early in his life. Whether heading out to apply for a job or take a final exam, just as the door was about to close behind him, his dad would call out, "Just have fun." Years later, Maharishi Mahesh Yogi, founder of TM®, said, "Life is bliss," and as a TM® teacher in the 1970s, David believed him.

David's Master's degree Advisors thought he should be a stand-up comic. Instead, he remained a lifelong healer, author, meditation teacher, and developer, creating 700+ products and programs founded in consciousness and wholeness. He spent decades studying Quantum Physics, consciousness, Unified Field Theory, and the best water balloon weapons available (Zuru Bunch O Balloons). He believes in "light-switch" solutions: rather than fight the dark, just flip the light-switch, and the darkness goes. Every one of his programs is completely effortless and simple — and they've helped millions whether they know it or not.

Conversation with David Adelson

Why are you excited about Quantum and Unified Field Physics?

David Adelson: I am excited about Quantum and Unified Field Physics because it helps us see the world's problems differently. Depending on how we look at problems, it causes us to stretch our brains and find creative solutions. Albert Einstein said that you couldn't solve a problem using the thinking level that created the problem. For example, many people are concerned about the oceans, the air, the environment — while other people are concerned about malnutrition and food issues. Others are concerned about stress and diseases such as COVID-19. People around the world are dealing with relationship issues and loneliness. We have no shortage of problems to solve.

The world is changing from Newtonian Physics to Quantum and Unified Field Physics. Newtonian Physics says a body in motion tends to stay in motion unless acted upon by an outside force. It is all about cause and effect — and relativity. Quantum and Unified Field Physics is an entirely different ballgame. With Quantum Physics, things come into being for no reason whatsoever. These "things" can move backward in time and then break apart and go off in opposite directions. Unified Field Physics is all possibilities because, according to science, the unified field is the source of everything, but it is unexpressed.

For example, It's just like water. There is potential for an ice sculpture in it, but we don't see that sculpture yet — it's unexpressed. The possibility is there — we just don't see it yet. But once it's been frozen and shaped, there it is. Just like that, everything we see — and hear and touch — in creation pre-exists in potential, unexpressed — unfrozen, unchiseled form. So, from the unified field, the potential is there for everything, for anything.

From the perspective of world problems, we can look at and solve the problems. For instance, people have developed rakes and nets to clean the oceans using the motion of waves. The materials would be caught and picked up to be moved somewhere else. That is one way to do it, but when we bring in the quantum level and the unified field level, the possibilities become limitless.

Think about this: instead of taking them and moving them somewhere, we could just dissolve them where they were and return them to their essential elements, which would nourish the planet. If we look at it from the quantum level, let's say we're living in the dark. There are no lights, and we've never heard of electricity. We're just in the dark. And every day, or every night, we walk a particular way, and we bang our shins.

We don't know what it is. We just bang it. We can't see what it is. We can't explore it. Then somebody comes along and flips on a light. Now, when we bang our shin, we can look down and see what it is. It's still there. We haven't changed it. It's still there. But because we can see it, we can now say, "Oh, I can just not walk there again. I don't have to make that mistake. I don't have to get hurt. It's like looking at it from a whole new level, maybe from the quantum level. From the unified field level, we can bring these "lights" to solve a lot of problems. In simple terms, we can think about what we want and get it. We can go beyond our limited thinking and create what we want now.

Once we have the light turned on, and we see the table that we've been banging our shin on, we don't have to move the table. We don't have to destroy the table. We just walk around it spontaneously. We just walk around it. The problem is solved without ever dealing with the situation.

So, with new technologies and new laws of nature that are becoming lively on the planet, what could have taken hundreds or thousands of years to shift in the world now can be done, in some cases, overnight. And I've seen extreme smog in LA in the 1970s disappear in 24 hours. Amazing things can happen. The truth is, we can create anything.

The unified field and quantum physics has all possibilities within it. We know that there are frequencies, tones, vibrations, or whatever we want to call it.

As a quantum and unified field inventor, we go in, and we find the frequencies that we want — health, joy, love — within the quantum field or unified field. Then we find or make something in the world that we can infuse with that energy and intelligence, for example, we may infuse them into a piece of art, an MP3, or a video program, or a pyramid for prosperity, or we teach people how to create it within themselves so that they can work with other people to clear things.

Over time, we have created more than 700 programs and tools for people to use to create whatever they want and need, such as peace, harmony, abundance, and so forth. Millions of people have benefited from my products, and many don't even know it.

Out of all these 700-plus programs that you've created, is there one that stands out that you're excited about?

David Adelson: Yes, there are two: The Peacemaker Systems have so much potential for so much good. People can sample the peacemaker system by downloading it at peaceandharmonydownload.com. It's very powerful.

The other is to eliminate money problems for everyone; called Magic Money Magnets, they fit in your pocket or purse and attract new, unexpected money and wealth to you. Who doesn't want more money? These are inexpensive and work miracles, hence the name, "Magic Money."

How do Quantum-Infused™ and Unified-Field-Infused™ programs work?

David Adelson: Using unique technology, we dive into the Quantum Field and Unified Field, locate the specific qualities we're looking for then draw them out like pulling a thread from a blanket. The thread stays connected, so the more we pull, the more of that quality comes out; unlike a blanket, these fields are limitless, so we never run out of the quality; there is no way we can "use them up": by definition, they are unlimited, infinite.

You know how big outer space is — it goes on for galaxies! It never ends. So, if we wanted to draw space like a thread into the atmosphere of earth, no matter how much space we pulled in, there is virtually unlimited space still left — it's huge.

Just like that, when we then infuse specific qualities within the field (such as peace, harmony, love, calm), our Quantum-Infused™ and Unified-Field-Infused™ programs create peace, love, and harmony drawing from the quantum and unified fields. So, no matter how much you use our programs, you cannot "use it up."

These programs and our new platforms have been created after 40+ years of research and study. At Peace & Harmony Co., we offer more than 700 easy-to-use Quantum-Infused™ and Unified-Field-Infused™ products and programs for love, joy, wealth, health, harmony, peace, success, faith, and trust, happiness, spiritual progress, fulfilling your life's goals and purpose, and so much more.

What are some of the things a PeaceMaker System can do for humanity?

David Adelson: PeaceMaker systems generate peace, harmony, calmness, and dissolve or reduce stress, tension, hatred, anger, upset. Practically, that means they help reduce violent crimes, increase safety and protection, help people get along better, understand each other better, balance society so the racial or discriminatory conflicts resolve peacefully, reduce trauma, reduce customer complaints in your business and ease tension between family members, neighbors, and your entire community. Even traffic accidents should go down.

If you want to protect your family, yourself, and your community and have peace as your legacy, the PeaceMaker System helps your family feel safe because they are safe. As people use it, they report feeling safe and protected while generating peace and goodwill, and they feel an undoing of the stress and tension of hundreds of years in this country. Think about it? Wouldn't bringing peace to your neighborhood and community to be profound and inspiring legacy?

How is the PeaceMaker System delivered? Describe.

David Adelson: There are three versions of the PeaceMaker System. They include the PeaceMaker 10,000, PeaceMaker 14,000, or PeaceMaker 30,000 broadcast system. They are ready to plug in and play with our Quantum-Infused™ and Unified-Field-Infused™ based programs already in place. You don't need to download anything. Each system is brand new, transmuted from being a great laptop to becoming a Quantum-Infused and Unified-Field-Infused™ broadcast tower. These systems are completely pure, so they only generate peace and harmony, love and healing from profound creation levels. The Peace Maker Systems are not designed to be hooked up to the Internet or to use any other software other than the PeaceMaker System signals.

The PeaceMaker 10,000 is a dedicated peace generating system designed to help you generate good vibes in your home or office. It is excellent for those seeking a better relationship with their neighbors with a range of 10,000 people or 10 miles, whichever comes first.

The PeaceMaker 14,000 helps to unite people in your world up to 14,000 people or up to an area of 15 miles, whichever comes first.

The PeaceMaker 30,000 creates real change and peace in the world around you! Help your family, friends, neighbors, and community stay safe in uncertain times. This system is specially designed for 30,000 people or 30 miles, whichever comes first.

How do you see the future of the world?

David Adelson: Things are getting better and better all the time.

I fully expect that we will have heaven on earth in the world because there are so many great well-wishers, especially in each subsequent generation. There are so many people, the younger generation, who already understand so much about the way things can be. Many social problems won't exist by the time they come into power. I think this is a fantastic time in the world. It is like a flower — the bud is destroyed so the flower can bloom.

It's a really exciting time to be alive. It's a really exciting time to participate from the level of joy and love and just well-wishing ourselves and others.

There is so much good going on now. I appreciate it. It's a wonderful gift to the divine to appreciate his or her creation.

Do you have an affiliate program?

David Adelson: We are very open to working with people who want to share our Peace and Harmony Company programs and products. Sign up at

PeaceAndHarmonyco.com/affiliate-area/

What is the best way to reach out to you?

David Adelson: You can experience the Peace and Harmony sample by downloading the video at

PeaceAndHarmonyco.com/sample/

About David Adelson

David Adelson is the lifelong healer and meditation teacher behind Peace and Harmony, a company dedicated to bringing serenity, hope, and transformation into the world. He has developed more than 700 unique Quantum-Infused™ and Unified-Field-Infused™ programs, including audio and video recordings, photography, and artwork, all designed to help people move with ease from a place of sadness, struggle, or frustration to one of good health, prosperity, and joy.

WEBSITE
PeaceAndHarmonyco.com

EMAIL
david@davidadelson.com

PODCAST
Here We Come to Save the Day
PeaceAndHarmonyco.com/Podcast

YOUTUBE
YouTube.com/user/HeavenCreating

FACEBOOK
Facebook.com/PeaceAndHarmonyCompany

LINKEDIN
LinkedIn.com/company/peace-harmony-co

INSTAGRAM
Instagram.com/PeaceAndHarmonyco

Best Practices in Legal Recruitment

Jason Elias is the founder and CEO of Elias Recruitment, a legal recruitment specialist, placing legal professionals into legal roles Australia-wide.

A thought leader and disrupter in the recruitment industry, Jason has won multiple awards including the 2020 RCSA Industry Award for Recruitment Leader of the Year.

This is what the judges said:

Jason Elias FRCSA has owned and managed a recruitment business for 20 years achieving impressive results. His leadership has seen many professionals join and stay in his business, having created a diverse environment which could be described as open, flexible, inclusive and collaborative.

He has been described as a leader "...who brings everyone along..."

Jason has made significant contributions to the industry, often involved in learning and leadership initiatives, sharing his knowledge.

Jason has worked collaboratively with stakeholders, internal and external, promoting the professionalism of the recruitment industry.

More recently, Jason won the coveted TIARA Australia - THE ENTIRE SOFTWARE BUSINESS LEADER OF THE YEAR. This particular award recognises a visionary recruitment leader who has achieved exceptional growth, pioneered transformational improvement – in their business and industry – and inspired the highest levels of engagement and performance from their people.

Conversation with Jason Elias

What is your value proposition for clients looking for help to fill legal positions?

Jason Elias: We have over 20 years of expertise as dedicated legal recruitment specialists, where we have helped legal professionals obtain in-house legal roles as well as moving successfully within their existing practices. So we are a safe pair of hands for anyone exploring their next legal career transition. As a baseline, we can offer expert insight into matching your career ambitions with any legal career opportunities that are available.

Additionally, Elias Recruitment is a veteran member of the NPAworldwide recruitment network that operates globally. Because we are the sole legal recruitment agency in Sydney as a member of NPAworldwide, our candidates have an unfair competitive advantage with potential access to over 1500 recruiters globally.

In helping match opportunities with career goals, we find that the following key questions are important to ask yourself before choosing a legal recruitment firm with to potentially partner with:

1. Are they a focused, dedicated legal recruitment firm that understands and appreciates the legal industry?

2. Am I actually liaising with an experienced, proven recruiter within that recruitment agency? Do they have their 10,000 hours of experience working in recruitment or even the legal world itself?

3. How long has the recruitment agency been established? Have they been able to develop the requisite relationships and partnerships in the legal industry to maximise your chances of success?

4. Does the recruitment firm have the capability of offering opportunities across a broad variety of geographies and industries, that suits your particular requirements and desires?

5. Is the recruitment firm an accredited RCSA member that subscribes to an industry-specific ethical code of conduct?

It's also worthwhile reminding yourself that it is often advantageous to partner with a single, proven recruitment leader that is capable of representing you across the industry.

Searching for new opportunities during COVID19 poses unique challenges. What would your advice be to job candidates who want to ace their next video interview?

Jason Elias: It goes without saying, as the COVID-19 pandemic continues, it makes sense to be well prepared for interviewing via Zoom, Microsoft Teams, or any of the other myriad videoconferencing tools being used.

We need to recognize and appreciate that the arrival of COVID-19 has meant fundamental shifts in how the recruitment process operates. This is no different for the legal recruitment process. Whether we like it or not, interviews via video have become the new norm and can often require a different approach than that of the conventional, run of the mill face-to-face interviews. Here are some useful strategies to help you ace your next job interview.

Appearance

Job interviewing 101 requires the presentation of a professional appearance. But interviews via video present some unique challenges to looking your absolute best. It may sound too obvious, but as a start, you should become familiar ahead of time with how the webcam hits you. Becoming comfortable with the visibility angles in advance, gives you an opportunity to plan on the ideal outfit that does not distract from the overlying technology. And do yourself a favour and resist the temptation to wear pyjamas, below what you *think* is the webcam viewing angle.

From recent personal experience, during one of my own video interviews, there was a moment when I needed to move from my initial set-up in middle of the interview, and I was glad I had decided to wear appropriate pants for the occasion.

Surroundings

Assuming you're conducting the interview remotely, the chances are that you will be doing this interview from the comfort of your home. But this comfort can be potentially dangerous.

Ideally, well ahead of the actual job interview, discover the best spot to set up your laptop or PC, as you want to be aware of what the interviewer may actually see in your background.

You also need to be aware of lighting. Sitting in front of a lovely bay window with the sun will give you a great view but will leave your interviewers looking at a dark silhouette.

There may also be an opportunity to show some additional personality in the interview, that would otherwise be impossible in face-to-face interviews. Something like a strategically placed memento like a University degree, picture of a pet or something similar. This of course is highly dependent on the culture of the company that is conducting the interview. Just make sure that whatever it is, that it is not too distracting.

If that isn't a possibility, then simply try and keep things simple and clean. It's important to remember that you are the focus and star of the occasion, not a messy living room, or noisy pets.

Videoconference tools

Without fail, almost every remote video meeting starts with something like "I can't hear you," or "Are you on mute?"

Technical problems can be very stressful, distracting and can even potentially ruin a video job interview.

Despite the fact that you aren't being recruited into a technology role, it's imperative to try and ensure that all the technical stuff is setup properly before-hand. It does not hurt to do a couple of dry runs, maybe with a friend or colleague to be sure that things like your microphone works as expected.

If the norm is that you are constantly competing with other household members for access to speed and bandwidth (have you met my kids?), negotiate with them beforehand to ensure that they are not attempting to download the entire internet during the actual interview.

Interviewers

COVID-19 hasn't changed everything though. Your home-work still starts long before the actual virtual interview.

Research and preparation are key. This includes the actual firm itself, its culture, any media mentions and so on, so that you can readily discuss these during the course of the interview. And beyond. In additional to this, the internet has made it super easy to become familiar with the actual interview panel before you meet them for the first time.

You may have noticed this already, but HR professionals and Partners are usually pretty active online, particularly on LinkedIn and a rudimentary search will help provide much needed background on those who you will be meeting virtually.

Make a lasting impression

These four strategies are essentially all about one main premise: making the best impression possible.

It is so easy to forget about the personal touches that can help make you stand out, when you are in the middle of a virtual interview. Keep in mind that non-verbal communication is so important that it makes up to 80% of the decision to move you forward in your application process.

Just ensure that you remain true to yourself and authentic, and this will undoubtedly help leave an impression that you are the right person for the position.

Ask good questions

It is a best practice to be prepared with a handful of questions to pose at the end of the interview when you are likely to be invited to do so. Importantly, try and avoid the usual "all-about-me" questions about benefits. On the contrary, try and show that you have actually listened to the interview panel. Position your questions to intimate that you are already successful in the application. Here are some examples:

- What are some of the things you like about working in this team/firm?

- In this role, what should success look like 6 months on?
- What's the best way of describing the culture of the group I would be joining?
- What might a typical day entail for this role/team?

In today's digital landscape, with the prevalence of social media, including LinkedIn, are CVs still relevant?

Jason Elias: I would say, very much so.

Whenever this type of question comes up in conversation, I usually refer to the study by **The Ladders,** an American Job Board that discovered that as a job candidate, you may only have 6 seconds to make an impact or you risk landing in the "Reject" pile. Recruiters generally focus on the following characteristics:

- Your name
- Your current role title and employer
- Length of time with your current workplace, and if still there
- Any previous roles with focus on names of firms and length of employment
- Bar admission date / any post-qualification experience
- Education – particularly for graduates.

Try to ensure that your CV lets a recruiter access this information readily to increase your chances of obtaining an interview. Don't be tempted with providing photos, logos, fancy fonts, and anything else that risks distraction. Always make sure that you fine-tune and tailor your CV to reflect the specified criteria of the role itself. If appropriate, make note of any complimentary experience and/or skills. Ideally, focus on any mention of past achievements in your most recent roles that readily match the role requirements.

Having said all that, here are four easy wins to improve your CV:

1. Employment History – Your work history should be listed in reverse chronological order and you should state clearly if you are still working. The following simple format works well:

Feb 2014- Name of current Law Firm, Sydney CBD Senior Partner

Duties include: (list 5-10 duties in bullet point format that are readily relevant to the role that you are applying for)

Achievements (list 3-5 achievements in bullet point format that easily highlight why you think you deserve an interview)

2. Keep it professional – Even if you think you look like Scarlett Johansson or George Clooney – rest assured that a photo is simply never appropriate on a legal CV. Try and keep all language formal and make sure to use the first person. It's advisable to ask someone to review the CV before clicking 'Send' – as it's not unusual for others to come across things like typos or similar that can be easily missed. Lastly, don't be afraid to let some of your personality show. This can be as simple as listing some interests or even hobbies.

3. Make it relevant – Can someone read your CV in less than 2 minutes? How easy would it be for total stranger to easily appreciate what value you brought to each position, your achievements, your strengths? When considering length, aim for 2 pages for a junior position and up to 4 pages for a more senior role. Focus on providing greater detail on your more recent positions. For example, if you have 10+ years PQE, then there isn't much need to know about your pre-legal roles with Bunnings. Certainly, mention it, of course but ensure that the focus is more on any relevant recent legal roles. Make sure to highlight any achievements you may have garnered in areas such as music, academia, public speaking, and sport for example.

4. Explain any short stints or gaps but don't embellish – Understand that it's easy for red flags to pop up for any unexplained absences or multiple roles that were short.

Obviously, there could be valid reasons and explanations including but not limited to; firm mergers, caring for family members, contract roles, or even perhaps following a partner on a lateral move. It is always better to have any of these explained appropriately on your CV rather than providing employers with the opportunity to arrive at their own conclusions and as a result, potentially prematurely ruling you out. And it goes without saying, whatever you do, do not lie. There is a real possibility that this would do immeasurable damage to your credibility and hurt your chances of securing any immediate opportunity. More so, it could even negatively affect your overall reputation moving forward with any future employers.

How do you advise candidates to position themselves in readiness for possible headhunter approaches?

Jason Elias: Head-hunters are quite methodical in their approach. Once they've been engaged, they tend to initially put feelers out via their established networks, then will compile a long list, then start researching candidates in that list to see who is likely to be a good fit. So, by the time they make an individual approach, they certainly know who they are, their work history and importantly what their reputation says about them.

So, if you want to maximise your chances of getting in their sights, there are 6 strategies that can help you achieve this.

Make social networks work for you, especially LinkedIn – Start by reviewing your personal LinkedIn profile, ensure that it represents your experience, expertise and area of practice, and clearly articulates your skillsets. Try and highlight your major engagements and focus on the value you believe you contributed (without breaching any client confidentiality, of course). Head-hunters by nature need to lock into the fact that you've worked on similar engagements to those they have been briefed about by their client. Don't be too modest, you can certainly blow your own horn.

Be recognised as an industry expert – Please understand that you'll never be approached by a head-hunter if no one has ever heard of you. So, if you're not already building an online profile for yourself, certainly start now.

Demonstrate your expertise whenever the opportunity presents itself, particularly for industry events or providing CPD.

Author content about important issues and hot button issues in your field influencing your work and share these insights far and wide. Don't rely on just your firm's newsletters for example, but directly with colleagues by posting and publishing on LinkedIn as well as other appropriate social media networks.

Catalysts for industry recognition can come in the form of simply joining some LinkedIn groups with like-minded professionals like the Australian Legal Community. Either start or continue contributing to relevant conversations. You could also consider publishing in wider media such as industry journals – or better yet, establish relationships with journalists to maximise opportunities of having quotes attributed to you in professional or even mainstream press as an expert in your industry.

Unleash subtle signals – If you are indeed considering new opportunities, it's definitely a good idea to start putting feelers out there. You could even change your personal LinkedIn privacy settings to discreetly show that you are open to new opportunities (which are not visible to your employer).

It's also possible to adjust your LinkedIn InMail settings allowing you to alert people that you are open to 'career opportunities.'

Make it easy for people to contact you, not a mystery – While receptionists are great gatekeepers who can easily shield you from those nasty telemarketing calls, they can also act as a hindrance for potential head-hunters who simply want to sound you out. So, make yourself as easy to contact as possible by including your mobile number, and your private email address within your LinkedIn profile. It's not difficult to appreciate that if a head-hunter finds it a struggle to get in contact with you, they may be tempted to simply bypass you and explore the opportunity with the next potential candidate on their list.

And if a head-hunter does call and connects with you, and you can't speak freely, simply arrange a convenient time to chat after office hours. This then gives you an opportunity to research their LinkedIn profile to see whether they are a good fit for a longer discussion.

Remain a true professional, don't breach etiquette – Make sure that you don't tell anyone in your firm – not a soul – about your intentions of moving on, even after having been approached. There is a danger that if the headhunting process isn't handled with discretion, you may likely jeopardise your existing employment and possibly any new potential opportunities as well.

Regardless of the temptation, if a head-hunter mentions the firm, do not approach the potential employer directly. Your inquiries will likely be met with blank stares, and you will certainly be seen as disloyal. They are employing a head-hunter for a reason and it may actually be a confidential search on many levels.

But don't be afraid – If you are ever subject to a head-hunter approach, you can definitely benefit from their experience and expertise. It never hurts to come across an insider source of industry intelligence, with recent knowledge of the state of the market. It is even more useful around performance/ salary review time. Even if this particular opportunity they intended on discussing doesn't work out, at least you've established a good industry relationship moving forward.

Finally, if you happened to have noticed that a head-hunter has viewed your LinkedIn profile, get in contact with them to find out why. The headhunting process can be likened to a slow dance of missed phone calls, personal profile views and overlooked messages sitting in your personal mailbox.

So, if you're open to new opportunities, stay alert and be responsive to any headhunting approaches.

What are some common questions you may be asked during legal job interviews?

Jason Elias: You may be presented with many different questions during a legal job interview. Here are some examples of some of the more common ones to help you in your preparation.

Questions regarding your experience

- What were your responsibilities/ accountabilities in your prior roles?
- What did you like about that position? Dislike?
- Why did you move on from your previous employment?
- While studying law, did you participate in any extracurricular activities?
- Do you consider your University results to be an honest indication of your academic capabilities?
- Do you think your University results are good indicators of your ability to rise to the challenge in this role?

Questions regarding your personality

- Tell us a little about yourself, perhaps something that may not be on your CV.
- How do you think your past colleagues and/or friends would describe you?
- As a person, how would you go about describing yourself.
- Do you have any extra-curricular hobbies or interests?
- Why did you attend law school / choose to practise law?

Questions regarding your strengths and weaknesses

- Describe one of your greatest achievements at any of your previous roles.
- What are your weaknesses/strengths?
- Do you prefer to work alone? Or are you a team player?

Conversely, what are some interview questions candidates should remember to ask their potential employer at the end of the interview?

Jason Elias: This is a great question because beyond a doubt this is the most overlooked aspect in most interviews. This potentially gives valuable insight to both the candidate and the interviewer.

Here are the main ones.

1. What would a typical day look like in this role? This isn't a placeholder question. At the end of the day, you really do want to be able to understand and appreciate what the role requires on a daily basis, to have a concise picture of the varied jobs you will be tasked with, who you will liaise and interact with, what tools or systems you might be exposed to, what challenges you can expect, what resources are available to you, and what skills and knowledge you will use regularly. This will certainly assist you in assessing whether indeed this role is a good match for your strengths and interests. Here are some examples of questions that will help you do this:

- What type of tasks would I be expected to fulfil on a daily basis?
- What matters could I be assisting with in this role?
- What proportion of my time would be allocated to autonomous tasks compared to team tasks?
- How would I recognise what success looks like in this role – six months down the road?

2. What is it like to be part of this firm? Together with understanding the tasks and responsibilities required in the role itself, you will want to also understand what the company culture is like. The work environment can be influenced in many ways, such as physical workspace, how the company is structured, how management is layered, whether the firm is big or small, and how different colleagues interact with each other. Companies often have on display their mission statements and values on their websites, and the interview is a ready opportunity to discover how this might resonate on a day-to-day basis. Think about questions like:

- What do you think are highlights for employees working here?
- How is important information from the leadership team shared?
- How would you describe the company culture?
- How beneficial do you think your company culture is? How does it differ from other law firms?
- Does the organisation actively support continuing professional development?

3. What is it like to be part of this team? Your immediate team, and its relevant interactions, plays a major part of any job. Especially your manager. Usually, you will have an opportunity during the recruitment process to meet the various associates or partners, and sometimes even meet with immediate team members. If this happens, take the opportunity to actively observe the team environment, and definitely pose a few questions as appropriate. Do remember that no team is perfect, they all have their strengths and weaknesses. So rather than seeking, and hoping for perfection, consider whether you will gain anything positive from working with this team, whether it could be fun, an appropriate challenge and a chance to develop new skills. You may want to consider asking questions such as:

- What are the current skill sets within this team?
- Does the team meet regularly? How often? What are they like?
- Can you give me an overview of the different roles within the team and how they interact together?
- What is your preferred management style with the team?

Jason, thank you for your advice for both job candidates and potential clients. What is the best way for people to get in contact with you?

The best way to be in contact is either connecting via LinkedIn, or via email Jason@eliasrecruitment.com.

Jason Elias

About Jason Elias: Jason Elias is a recent winner of the Australian Recruitment Leader of the Year at the RCSA awards. He is currently Chairman of the RCSA New South Wales/ACT regional Council and Global Chairman of NPA worldwide.

He was a previous winner of the NPA Chairman's Award. He is a qualified legal practitioner, fellow of the RCSA and currently undertaking a Master's in Legal Business Management.

About Elias Recruitment: Elias Recruitment is a legal recruitment specialist, placing legal professionals into legal roles Australia-wide. Founded in 2000, Elias Recruitment are headquartered in Sydney, and have consultants in Sydney, Melbourne, Brisbane and Perth.

Elias Recruitment

Suite 901, Level 9 84 Pitt Street
Sydney NSW 2000
Australia

PHONE
+61 2 9555 5711

EMAIL
info@eliasrecruitment.com

WEBSITE
EliasRecruitment.com

LinkedIn
au.LinkedIn.com/Company/Elias-Recruitment

Facebook
Facebook.com/EliasRecruitment

Twitter
Twitter.com/EliasRecruit